AF304892

Batch 427374UK00

427374UKX00355B	9781954597815	13 Haunted Ni
PERFECT	5.25X8.00	94
427374UKX00356B	9798827029755	She Is The Poe
PERFECT	5.25X8.00	118
427374UKX00357B	9798540242592	Did Not Finish
PERFECT	5.25X8.00	138
427374UKX00358B	9780999451984	Dirty Heads: A
PERFECT	5.25X8.00	144
427374UKX00359B	9781951570323	The Great Gats
PERFECT	5.25X8.00	162
427374UKX00360B	9781630518509	Map of the Sou
PERFECT	5.25X8.00	198
427374UKX00361B	9780998967172	The Remaking
PERFECT	5.25X8.00	218
427374UKX00362B	9789083004808	Corporate Reb
PERFECT	5.25X8.00	224
427374UKX00363B	9781777064907	What Young Ch
PERFECT	5.25X8.00	238
427374UKX00364B	9798364720719	Art-Horror: Th
PERFECT	5.25X8.00	254
427374UKX00365B	9781913891237	Picking Off Ne
PERFECT	5.25X8.00	266
427374UKX00366B	9781800801608	The Dead Call
PERFECT	5.25X8.00	288
427374UKX00367B	9798987266625	What's Left of
PERFECT	5.25X8.00	290
427374UKX00368B	9781800800090	Kill Our Sins
PERFECT	5.25X8.00	300

ISBN	Title	Pages	Finish	Qty
81950413195 50X8.25	My Lover Feeds Me Grapefruit	90	MATTE	(1)
83752431063 3X8.27	Jessica's First Prayer. Jessica's Mother	68	MATTE	(1)
83752330274 3X8.27	A Narrative of Service With the Third Wi	84	MATTE	(1)
80715142028 3X8.27	Church of England Marriage Services: Wit	96	MATTE	(1)
83752338553 3X8.27	Hymns of the Early Church	100	MATTE	(1)
83752411256 3X8.27	VC - a Chronicle of Castle Barfield and o	104	MATTE	(1)
83752332315 3X8.27	The Ascent of Man	120	MATTE	(1)
83752343441 3X8.27	Sir Charles Napier	132	MATTE	(1)
83752332346 3X8.27	Bikey the Skicycle and Other Tales of Jim	136	MATTE	(1)
83752417203 3X8.27	The Rocky Mountain Wonderland	146	MATTE	(1)
83752344370 3X8.27	The Border Boys on the Trail	148	MATTE	(1)
83752424010 3X8.27	Change in the Village	156	MATTE	(1)
83752338010 3X8.27	Ned in the Block-House	158	MATTE	(1)
83752326147 3X8.27	The Infidel :Volume 1	168	MATTE	(1)

h 427374UK00004B

83752326390	Original Penny Readings, A Series of Shor		
3X8.27	200	MATTE	(2)
83752330014	Bungay Castle:Volume 1		
3X8.27	202	MATTE	(1)
81910935927	Steampunk International		
3X8.27	204	MATTE	(1)
83750409545	Shadow Disease chronic active Toxoplasm		
3X8.27	270	MATTE	(1)
81932195194	A God in the House: Poets Talk about Fai		
3X8.27	306	MATTE	(1)

Milton Keynes UK
Ingram Content Group UK Ltd.
UKHW011939230823
427374UK00004B/250